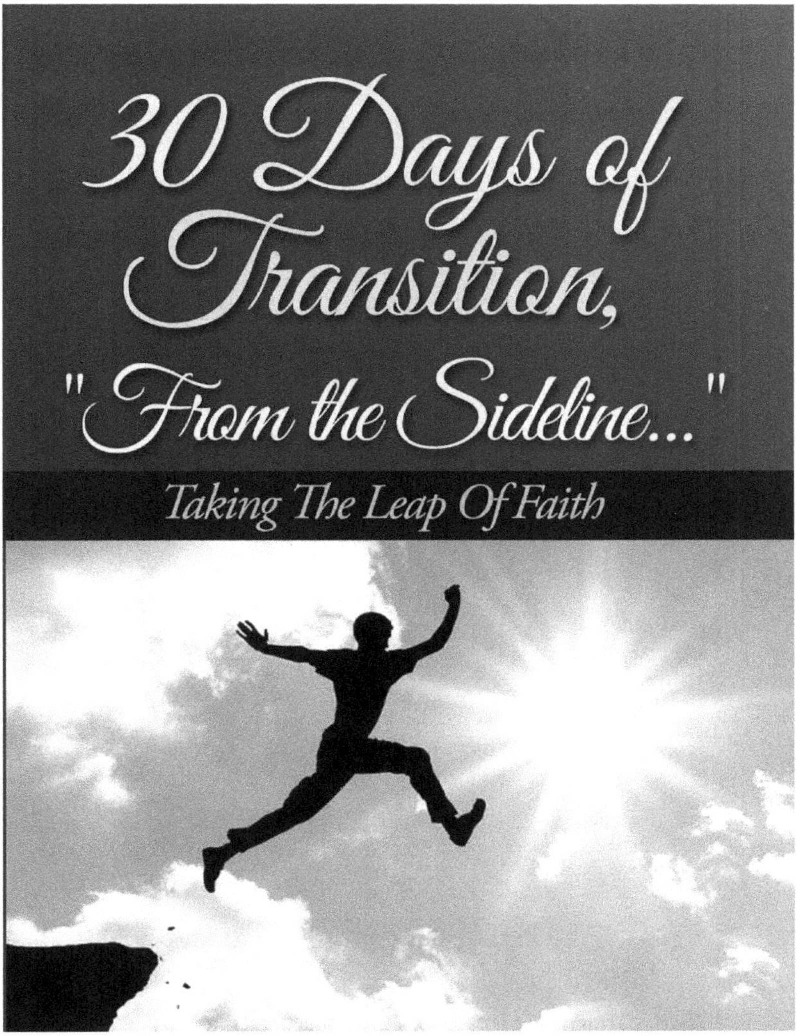

30 Days of Transition,
"From the Sideline..."
Taking The Leap Of Faith

Copyright © 2016 by Kim M. Martin, CTACC
All rights reserved.

ISBN-10: 0692475621
ISBN-13: 9780692475621

DEDICATION

*This book is dedicated to those who were brave enough
to take a leap of faith in order to live out their
life's passion and purpose.
It is a difficult journey, but it is worth it!*

Acknowledgements

30 Days of Transition, From the Sideline… is the second book in my 3-book "From the Sideline" series. This book is special to me, not only because it is my sophomore book, but because I've made a few transitions while this book was being written. Many of these pages were written as a result of my experiences. The journey has not been without its twists and turns, but I have had some awesome people who have been by side through it all.

I would like to acknowledge three very special people at this time. Without them, I would not have been able to experience transition in such a positive way. Jerrod has been the love of my life for the past 5 years. He has supported me in my goals and aspirations with love. He has given me the space to be creative and to flesh out what I wanted my business model to look like. He has also played the devil's advocate and asked the tough questions that needed to be asked in order to prompt me to justify WHY I do what I do. I believe I needed this balance in order to remain grounded. Jerrod, I will always love you for attempts to love me unconditionally.

Sheronda Barksdale is the newest person to enter my life, but one who has had the greatest impact. I met Sheronda at a vision board party she was hosting, and we have been inseparable ever since. We combined our individual businesses to create Unlimited Love and Life Coaching, LLC, and launched our Blog Talk Radio show, Love Unlimited: Relationship Coaching with Kim and Sheronda. She came at a time when I was rebranding my business and trying to define what the message of my business was going to be. The story behind my business was there, but the message was unclear. Sheronda helped me to define my message and then partnered with me to make it come into fruition. Her creativity and my initiative, coupled with our ability to complete each other's sentences, have made us fast friends and effective business partners. She is my sister and I love her. I know that there will be so many more successes to come as a result of our willingness to collaborate and not compete with one another. Thank you Sheronda for your commitment to our business and our partnership.

I want to also take a moment to acknowledge a very, very special person to me. She has been with me all of my life and will be with me even when God calls her home. She is my grandmother, **Martha Pass**. She has been my biggest fan since the day I was born. Our birthdays are a day apart and we have always had the chance to celebrate life together. In her eyes, I have always been a star. She has always told me how proud she was of me and I always believed her. She is irreplaceable. I love her with all my heart. She is my Nana.

"Nana...thank you for always loving me. Thank you for showing me who God is through your actions and through your words. I will always make you proud and represent our family, by carrying on your legacy. I love you!"

I would be remiss if I did not give a "special shout out" to
Dorothy Pass
Auntie Dottie, you will ALWAYS be
"MY FAVORITE AUNTIE IN THE WHOLE WIDE WORLD!!"

I would also like to acknowledge all my family member and friends who continue to be in my corner, cheering me on. You continue to believe in my ability to follow my dreams and to succeed. I love each of you INFINITY for that! Keep watching...I'm not done!

TABLE OF CONTENTS

Day 1 – "D-Day" ………………………………………… 9
Day 2 – "Be Prepared" …………………………………… 11
Day 3 – "Tying Up Loose Ends" ………………………… 13
Day 4 – "The Morning After" …………………………… 15
Day 5 – "No Regrets…Well…Maybe" ….……………… 17
Day 6 – "Time Is of the Essence" ……………………… 19
Day 7 – "Support System…Check!" …………………….. 21
Day 8 – "Healthy Mind, Body & Spirit" ……………….. 23
Day 9 – "The Disconnect" ……………………………… 25
Day 10 – "Emotional Rollercoaster" ……………………27
Day 11 – "Confidence" ………………………………….. 29
Day 12 – "Explore Other Interests" ……………………. 30
Day 13 – "Ask for Help" ………………………………… 31
Day 14 – "Stay The Course" ……………………………. 32
Day 15 – "The ½ Way Mark" …………………………... 33
Day 16 – "Encouragement" ………………….…………... 34
Day 17 – "Take A Day Off" …………………………… 35
Day 18 – "Live Authentically" ………………………… 36
Day 19 – "Money Matters"..……………………………. 37
Day 20 – "In the Zone" ………………………………... 38

Day 21 – "Letting Go" 39
Day 22 – "Being Present" 41
Day 23 – "Nobody Can Be You" 42
Day 24 – "Don't Recreate the Wheel" 43
Day 25 – "Write Your Own Chapter" 44
Day 26 – "Be a Person of Integrity" 45
Day 27 – "Experience Gratitude" 46
Day 28 – "RedeFINDing You 47
Day 29 – "The Manifestation" 48
Day 30 – "Transformation" 49

Day 1– "D – Day"

It's "D – Day"! You have finally realized that a change needs to happen in your life. You may have said one or more of the following statements:

- I've been *DEALING* with my situation for too long
- I'm *DONE* compromising myself for others
- I have *DECIDED* that I am worth more than the situation I'm in
- The line of *DEMARCATION* has been drawn for what I am willing to tolerate and no one is allowed to cross that line anymore
- I no longer allow others to *DICTATE* how I choose to live my life
- I am no longer *DEFINED* by the role I play in other people's lives
- "The *DEVIL* is a liar!"

You are now ready to say with confidence:

- I have *DISCOVERED* my passion and my purpose
- I have *DEVELOPED* a plan for my life and am ready to execute it
- I am *DETERMINED* to live my life authentically
- I am ready to walk in my *DESTINY*
- I am ready to make *DEFINITIVE* changes in my life so I can experience the fullness of my passions and my purpose
- I am *DRIVEN* to accomplish my goals because I have surrounded myself with positive, supportive people
- I have an overwhelming *DESIRE* to just *DO* it!

Have you given your transition a **DATE**? Have you **DECIDED** on a particular **DAY** that you want to set the wheels in motion to move from where you are to where you want to go?

If you haven't, how about making TODAY that day! If you don't become **DEFINITIVE** about the changes you want to make in your life, you will **DISCOVER** that time has passed and you haven't gone anywhere. Major life transitions are about movement. **DISCIPLINE** yourself so that you don't lose focus of your goals.

You have a passion and a purpose stirring inside
of you that is ready to be birthed.
It is time to DELIVER it!

Day 2 – "Be Prepared"

There are a few things to keep in mind as you prepare to make major life transitions. Here are a few questions you need to ask yourself: Have you written out a step-by-step plan for what you want to do over the next 3-12 months? Have you prepared/planned financially for this change? Have you researched and/or consulted with someone regarding any grey areas you may have as you transition? Do you have your support system in place for those times when you may need encouragement or inspiration? Having a plan in place will give the transition in your life DIRECTION.

Think of it as your "internal navigation system". In order to get to where you're going, you have to first have a destination. If you don't know where you're going, you will wind up in a constant state of "recalculating". Your wheels will be in motion, but won't be sure where you'll end up. You definitely don't want to go down a dead end or into a bad area of your life where you've already been. The goal is to have a destination set and to begin to travel toward that destination. Now this is not to say that it won't take some time to get there, or that there may not be some obstacles along the way. The goal is to be prepared, so when those obstacles come along, you have the tools you need to address them.

The purpose of creating a 3 to 12- month plan is so it can implemented IMMEDIATELY. I purposely made this a short-term goal, so it is attainable. Notice that I did not say 3- to 5-year plan. Some of us are intimidated by creating a plan so far in the future. To be honest, some of us aren't sure about what we want to do next week! In the words of Creighton Abrams, "When eating an elephant, take one bite at a time!" Writing out short-term goals will give you the confidence to plan in smaller time frames until you are able to build up to longer-termed ones. Financial planning is another step that is paramount, especially if you are transitioning from a job or a long term-relationship. Having your finances in order will make the transition smoother because it gives you leverage and can minimize some of the unexpected events that can {and will} arise.

Doing your research and consulting with a coach, counselor or mentor will help to avoid unnecessary roadblocks. The more you know, the easier it is to maneuver through the unexpected. Don't be afraid to ask for HELP! This is the information age. We have several resources available to us. USE THEM. If there is something you are interested in and it is in alignment with your vision or purpose, investigate it. See if there is more that you can do to further expand your plan. Finally, evaluate who is in your circle of influence. Make sure that the ones selected have EARNED their place in your circle by supporting your purpose and vision. They should encourage and empower you and be willing to "ride" with you when your journey gets a little rough. Before you "leap", take the time to be prepared.

Following these few basic steps will minimize the "recalculations" that are sure to take place, but will still help you reach your destination towards your purpose and your vision.

Day 3 – "Tying Up Loose Ends"

Now that you have made the decision to make a transition in your life, you need to go through the process of tying up loose ends. You don't want anything to hinder your ability to move forward. This means taking care of your affairs so that you won't have to go back or possibly be drawn back into your previous situation. If you are making a career change and leaving your current position, have you asked all of the questions you needed to or signed off on all of the paperwork pertaining to your benefits packages? Do you know how long your medical, dental and vision policies will last after your last day of employment? Do you have a copy of your separation notice and/or any other documents or certificates you may be entitled to?

If you are ending a long-term relationship, do you have any bank accounts or leases that are in both of your names? Have you changed that person as an emergency contact or beneficiary on a policy you may have? Do you have any outstanding debt or property that you own together that needs to be legally divided? These are just a few of the questions you may want to address before you make your bold move toward transition. You don't want to take three steps forward only to have to take two steps back due to unresolved issues. You always want to make a clean break. If you feel like you've made a mess, do what you would do if you physically made one. Take the time to clean it up! Make sure no evidence of the "mess" is left, so that area of your life is restored. It will make for a smoother transition.

I would be remiss if I didn't say that sometimes tying up loose ends isn't easy. Sometimes you may be required to keep the lines of communication open, especially in a relationship where a child may be involved or in a family business where you may still have to interact with family members. What needs to be established here, is the best form of communication for all parties involved. You have to consider whether this is something you can handle civilly or if it needs to be established legally. A key step in being able to transition successfully is to be true to yourself and others. If you already know that the situation is going to cause tension, take the steps necessary to relieve as much of that tension as possible. If you are not sure how to accomplish that, ask for help and seek advice from someone who does. Volatile situations don't absolve themselves. Taking the initiative to create a positive space for you to interact with the person, will allow you to move forward without losing momentum.

      The ultimate goal of tying up loose ends is to create closure. Closure brings about peace. Peace gives you a sense of freedom. The release that comes from being free, gives you the confidence you need to walk boldly in the next steps toward your journey to transition. There are no longer those unresolved issues that will take you back to a place you worked so diligently not to return to. Tying up loose ends will put you on track towards your passion and purpose, with no obstacles and a clear path ahead.

Tying up loose ends helps us to resolve issues where we seek closure and FREES us to move forward on the path toward our passion and purpose!

Day 4 – "The Morning After"

Today is the first day of your NEW BEGINNING! How do you feel? Are you ready to jump out of the bed and spring into action? Or are you having second thoughts? The day after any major transition in your life can be one of the toughest. You are excited about what the day will bring, but also apprehensive about what to expect. What if the day doesn't turn out the way you imagined? Will you feel the urge to run back to that familiar comfort zone you have become so accustomed to? All of these questions will be swirling around in your head, but the one thing you want to do is remain FOCUSED. By now, some planning and preparing for your transition has taken place. You have attempted to tie up any loose ends that may have caused delays. The thing to remember is NOT TO PANIC. As with anything new, you will encounter some anxiety. That is perfectly normal. Turn that anxiety into positive energy that will help you navigate through your day with confidence. So what now? It's the morning after...

Remember that you are taking a step in the right direction. You have taken one more step in your journey toward your vision and your purpose. You should feel that little twinge of excitement similar to what you feel when you are starting a new job or a new relationship. Those butterflies in your stomach and feelings of euphoria you feel when something just feels "right". It should be a release...confirmation that you are doing what is best for YOU. Now is the time to begin implementing your plan and developing a daily routine. Establishing routines early on, will keep you on task and eliminate any feelings of overwhelm.

My daily routine starts with meditation and prayer, followed by the writing down of my intentions for the day. Meditation and Tai Chi centers and mentally prepares me for the day's activities. Having my intentions written out for the day ensures that I accomplish my tasks based on priority. I then go about carrying out my tasks for the day, making sure that I leave time in my schedule for the unexpected. I end each day by writing down three things I am grateful for. Ending each day with gratitude allows me to reflect on the positive experiences I had and prepares me for my time of prayer before going to bed.

A solid routine creates healthy habits. You will find that you can rebound from any situation when you are prepared and focused. It's all about the execution of your plans now. The goal is to keep the momentum going. If you allow fear to take over, it will paralyze you and you won't even make it out of the bed! The more consistent you are in implementing your plans, the more confidence you will gain on the path toward your passion and purpose.

It's the morning after...start implementing your plan and developing a routine TODAY!

Day 5 – "No Regrets...Well...Maybe..."

So... it's been a few days and things haven't changed in the monumental way you thought they would. Feelings of doubt and regret have begun to enter into your spirit. "Why did I do this?" "Did I hear God right?" "Why haven't things begun to manifest already?" These are the common questions that arise when we make major life transitions. We want our decision to make a change to be met with instant gratification and we want it NOW!

The reality is that patience and an unwavering faith need to become a daily part of your life. Although we make plans and preparations for the changes we want to make in our lives, they don't always happen instantly. Life changes are a process. They happen over time. Think of the relationships you have been in. It took time to cultivate them and to establish a level of comfort before you took things to the next level. Think about your first day on a new job. It took time to learn the things you were unfamiliar with and to get acclimated to the job and your new responsibilities. These things took time...but they were worth it. Your patience will pay off.

Now DOUBT will take on a liquefied state and get into every nook and cranny of your psyche. You will experience extreme emotional highs and lows before things fall into place. There will be days when it seems like everything is going great for everyone BUT you! Life will seem unfair and you will begin to think that things will never change. Some of you will even go so far as to challenge God and ask Him how long He intends to make you suffer! There will be days when things will appear hopeless. When moments of doubt arise, remember that your situation had to change in order for your vision to manifest itself. You may have had to walk away from a job in order for your time to be freed up to pursue your new venture. You may have had to end a relationship so that the opportunity for another to develop could take place. All of these things take place as a part of your journey. The key word here is JOURNEY.

Take comfort in knowing that you are on your path to GREATNESS. Learn to focus on those things you are grateful for. Consider keeping a gratitude journal and writing down the things you are grateful for each day. When those "down days" arise, go to your journal and reflect on the good things that were taking place, while you were focusing on the bad. You may discover that things are not as bad as you thought they were. Keeping a positive attitude will manifest into positive energy. The positive energy you send out will be received and sent back to you. Be careful not to get so caught up in doubt and negative thoughts, that you miss the blessings that may be coming your way. What is meant for you will come in its perfect time. When you feel like giving up, take time to remember why you started your journey in the first place. Let that motivate you to keep moving forward. Never forget the purpose for following your vision. There was a reason it was given to you. Continue to walk in faith and be patient in receiving your blessings. Use this time to prepare yourself for the overflow that is coming. It may be closer than you think!

Having patience and remaining faithful to your vision will eliminate any feelings of doubt. Stay the course!

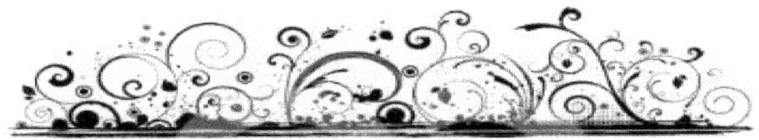

Day 6 – "Time Is of the Essence"

Time management is paramount when transitioning into anything new. How you maximize your time will determine how effective you will be in accomplishing your goals. It will also minimize the feelings of overwhelm you feel when your "to-do list" is longer than you anticipate. More importantly, you want to be sure that personal time and flex time are incorporated into your schedule so that a balance is created.

The common misconception regarding time management is that it's about managing time. Time management is really about productivity. It is your ability to prioritize your tasks so that the most important ones are getting done in a timely manner. We all have tasks that we want to accomplish during any given day. If we don't take the time to write them down and prioritize them, then we leave those tasks up to our memory. If your memory is like mine, you won't even remember why you tied that string around your finger! It is best to create a system that works best for you. An old-fashioned Franklin Planner works for me! Some may choose to use an electronic planner or a combination of both. Whatever your method, choose one that is portable and easily accessible.

We have to be intentional about the things we HAVE to do, so that can incorporate the things we WANT to do into our lives. There are some tasks we can wait on and others we can't. Is it in your best interest to miss your doctor or dentist appointments? What about those for your children? Or that interview for a new job? An important meeting regarding your business? What about your anniversary or a family member's birthday? Categorizing your tasks by level of importance, allows the wiggle room needed to shift things around that can wait for another day. It is best to try to schedule your high priority tasks first, so that you have a better chance of getting them done before the day slips away.

Flexibility in our schedules also allows for the unexpected. I incorporate exercise into my day, as my work and research can have me sitting for hours at a time. I need at least 30 minutes to move around and stretch my body. I also incorporate 20-30 minutes of meditation into my day so that I have the mental breaks I need as well. If an unexpected event should arise, I now have an hour where I can shift activities if I need to. I don't forfeit the things I want to do. I simply shift them by moving a task that can wait, to the following day.

One thing you will learn as you begin to master time management is that another person's "emergency" is not yours. The hours in your day can easily be absorbed by other people's drama. We have to be able to determine when a situation is one that we need to be involved in or not. If not, we need to learn to say "NO", so we can get back to the business of carrying out our plans for the day. It is the sacrifice we have to be willing to take in order to avoid feelings of guilt and feelings of overwhelm when we don't achieve our goals for the day. We have to be willing to stay the course, and where we fall short, pick ourselves up and forge ahead until we create better time management skills that we can implement for a lifetime!

Time management isn't about time, it's about productivity.

Day 7 – "Support System…Check!"

     Having a strong support system as you go through any life transition makes all the difference in the world! When doubt, anxiety and feelings of overwhelm try to attack, it nice to know you have a "support team" behind you to fight off any negative thoughts that come your way. Those who have been SELECTED to be in your inner circle, will not have that "crabs-in-a-barrel" mentality. They will never seek to pull you down. They are always finding ways to encourage you and empower you in those things you are aspiring to do. They are not envious. Any suggestions or comments they make regarding the things you are doing, are made out of pure love. When you are sharing your ideas or spending time with them, they are PRESENT. They actively listen and give you the impression that what you are saying has merit. You can feel that they truly value your relationship.

     These are the characteristics that should be evident when you think about those in your inner circle. There should be no trepidation when it comes to any members of this very special and personal group of individuals. The individuals in your inner circle should not only be selected by you, but they should EARN that place in your life. There will be people who will come into your life for various reasons. Some will be for the right reasons, and some will be for selfish gain. It is our discerning spirit and history with that person, that will determine which category they fall into, and the role they will play in our lives. This can take time to establish. There are however instances where you "click" with a person and you wind up being life-long friends. Sometimes it's a family member who loves and supports you just because you're "family".

     No matter the reason, when that support system is firmly in place, you feel unstoppable! Even when you feel like you can't operate in your own abilities, you know that you have people around you that will step in and hold you up, until you can stand on your own feet again. They are there when you feel defeated and will rally behind you until your next "win". Time is not a factor because no matter how long it takes, they will be there at the finish line, cheering you on. There is no greater feeling…

The one thing that we have to keep in mind is that there are those of us who feel like we don't have that support system. We feel like it is us against the world. How are we supposed to move forward when we feel like WE are all we have? If you take away nothing else from the words written in this book, remember that YOU are not alone. There is ONE that is always working for your good. Seen and unseen. The greatest support system you have in your life is YOU, governed by the ONE you believe in. Faith is an integral part of transitioning. The faith you had to believe you could make the positive changes you are making in your life, is that same faith that will allow you to push through when things get tough. When you feel that others are not around, reach deeper within yourself and tap into that same source that allowed you to take the steps you took in the first place. The ONE that you believe in. Meditation and prayer can create that space to accomplish the peace and support you desire. It begins with YOU.

Support systems are amazing!
They are all about choices, and those choices begin with YOU!

Day 8 – "Healthy Mind, Body & Spirit"

Proper Sleep, good nutrition and strong faith are key factors in making significant transitions in your life. They provide the balance and energy we need to function properly on a daily basis. They also keep our immune systems and overall health running at optimal levels. When we take the time to take care of ourselves, we benefit from the overall sense of wellness it creates.

I learned this lesson the hard way when I decided to transition from my corporate position. I was excited that I finally took the leap of faith to pursue my own business. I also decided that it would be an opportune time to pursue my doctoral degree. Instead of taking some time to rest and properly prepare my mind, body and spirit for my transition, I immediately registered for school, started attending all kinds of networking events. I accepted any speaking engagements that came my way. I did not want to miss any opportunities to promote my business. I was ready to conquer the world!

Within two weeks, I hit the proverbial "brick wall". In my eagerness to be everywhere and do everything, I quickly began to feel the negative effects of my ways. I was attending networking events all hours of the day, and writing and researching papers all hours of the night. I was getting very little sleep and was eating sporadically. My once established exercise regimen was non-existent. I had no energy and was gaining weight quickly. My habits were affecting not only my work, but my health. I soon realized I had to do something different or suffer the consequences.

I had to re-evaluate how I conducted myself on a daily basis. I had to learn to break for meals and take time to engage in an exercise regimen, as I had done in the past. I had to incorporate time for meditation and prayer. I had to go back to those things that worked for me prior to my transition.

With my newfound career and educational goals, I knew those good habits I had, simply had to change to fit my new lifestyle. I sat down and planned out my days to incorporate time for meals, prayer, meditation and exercise. I also tried my best to end my days early enough to get the rest my body needed. This was done with the understanding that at times my schedule might change. When I was not able to sit for a meal, I carried healthy snacks. When I did not have time for a 30-minute exercise routine, I would park further away to get in a short walk. I would take five minutes in the car to control my breathing as a form of meditation. I even tried to take a power nap in the middle of the day. I wanted to give myself parameters to work within, so that my life had some semblance of order. When I achieved this, my energy returned, I felt a sense of wellness again and my confidence levels rose as well. I was ready, once again, to conquer the world…only smarter this time!

When transitioning, we have to be mindful of those things that will help us to remain on the path toward our vision, plan and purpose. This includes eating properly, doing some form of exercise, getting restorative rest, and having time for meditation and prayer. Our bodies are our temples and we need to take care of them. When we take care of our mind, body and spirit, we can be the vessels used to empower and inspire others.

Let's choose to love ourselves, by taking care of ourselves.

Day 9 – "The Disconnect"

     You have finally made the transition from that job or relationship that needed to end. You feel as though you have finally severed the ties that had you bound to that job or that person. You are feeling confident in your decision and are ready to move on with your life. Things are finally looking up! But then you realize that there is a force that keeps pulling you back to the place you fought so hard to transition from. That force is coming from your ex-coworkers or the mutual friends of your ex-significant other.

     When I resigned from my corporate position, my former coworkers and I promised to keep in touch, and we did. The conversations would begin with, "Hey girl! I miss you" and "How are you doing?" But it would quickly turn into a gripe session about the job. "Girl, guess what happened?" "Let me tell you what so-and-so did." "This place is driving me crazy!" Although their intentions were good, I realized that each call was becoming one of two things; a coaching session for them and a soul tie for me. I found myself giving advice and suggestions on what they needed to do, and I also found myself trying to problem solve the things that were going on in the office.

     What finally made me realize that I had to do something about this, was a call I received from one my closest friends there. She was explaining to me some of the changes that were being made by management and I found myself getting upset. I said, "How are we going to revise our review to reflect these changes?" I was no longer working there and I said "WE"… This is when I realized I was still tied to the place I thought I had successfully walked away from. My relationship with my ex-coworkers was not allowing me to move forward. It was holding me back.

     Making transitions in our lives may require us to re-evaluate our relationships. If the relationship is going to consistently keep us connected to that person or place we successfully transitioned from, then we have to be willing to alter or completely let go of that relationship. I did not leave my job to be told every move they made since I left. If I was interested, I would have stayed there. I needed to sever the ties that had me bound.

The same is true with relationships where you and your ex-significant other have mutual friends. Every time you speak to that friend, you don't want them constantly telling you what your ex is doing or who they are seeing. You have moved on from the relationship and don't need to be bound to that person through your friend. I don't believe that their intention is to hurt you. They simply don't realize that it took a great effort to transition from that relationship and you need to keep the momentum going forward…not backwards.

The important thing to remember here is that you have to find a new common ground within in your relationships, whether personal or professional. If you leave a job or end a relationship, realize that if you can't establish a commonality outside of the situation you left, then it may be time to "disconnect"…

Be sure that the relationships you have with those in your past, don't keep you bound to your past. Re-evaluate those relationships and disconnect if necessary. Choose to move forward.

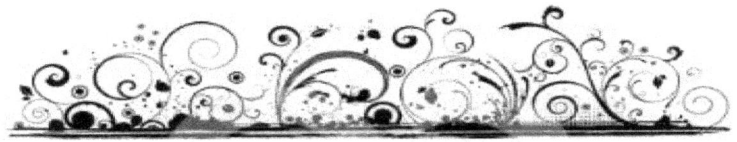

Day 10 – "Emotional Rollercoaster"

I love rollercoasters! Being from New York and riding the rollercoaster at Coney Island is one of my fondest memories. The speed, dips, sharp turns and loops were exhilarating. I would strap in, with excitement mounting, and off I went! A few minutes later, it was over. I enjoyed it so much that I found myself looking around for the next thing that produced that same feeling. Physical rollercoasters are fun, but emotional ones are a different animal.

As you make transitions in your life, you will find yourself riding on an emotional rollercoaster more often than you care to admit. There will be days when you feel like you can conquer the world. It will seem like the stars have aligned and you are in "the zone". Other days you will wonder why you even got out of the bed. Sometimes it will feel like everything that could go wrong…did! The ride can vary from day to day. The emotional highs and lows can be hard to comprehend and just as hard to deal with.

The one thing that helps me deal with my emotions, is living my life with gratitude. I end each day listing three things that I am grateful for. It causes me to focus on the positive things that have taken place each day. It also gives me a fresh perspective on the things that are happening in my life. When I go back and read the things I am grateful for, I see that my situation is not as bad as I thought it was.

Meditation is another way to deal with fluctuating emotions. Being able to take a moment to center and refocus your mind, releases any anxieties you may be experiencing. Meditation also gives you the clarity needed to determine what your next steps should be in any given situation. Meditation can be restorative and can create calm in the midst of chaos.

Journaling is a great outlet we can use when our emotions are running high. It is a great way to document our "wins" when we are having a productive day. But it is also a good way to release our frustrations when we are having a more challenging day. If we can release our frustrations on paper, we are giving ourselves an opportunity to visualize where our frustration lies. If we are angry with someone or about something, we can write out what we want to say about the situation without damaging the relationship. We can then decide the best way to deal with the situation. Is it best to address the person or situation with our concerns or do we simply throw the paper away?

Transition will take you on quite an emotional ride. Make sure that you take the steps to secure yourself for all of the twists and turns it will take. Hold on tight and know that these emotional times will be over before you know it.

__Having an outlet to express our feelings helps up to better cope with emotional highs and lows.__

Day 11 – "Confidence"

Dictionary.com defines confidence as "a feeling of self-assurance arising from one's appreciation of one's own abilities or qualities." When we choose to follow the path toward our life's passion and purpose, it requires us to be confident. That confidence allows us to step outside of our comfort zone and try something new.

If someone would have told me 2 years ago that I would have my own business, be a 4-time published author, professional speaker, and blog talk radio co-host, I would have looked around to see who they were talking to! I was content working my corporate job and living my routine life. I knew I had talents, but wasn't interested in pursuing them. However, the more time passed, the more opportunities arose for me to use my talents.

With each opportunity, came more opportunities. People began to ask me why I wasn't coaching or speaking to individuals who wanted to hear what I had to say. They began to ask why I hadn't written a book about some of the things I had experienced. After a while, their "whys" became my "why not?" Why didn't I pursue these things? When I couldn't answer that question, I began to ask myself, "why should I?" What I realized is that I could do these things and I wanted to do them because I had a passion for helping people transition and "redeFIND" themselves. I began to gain confidence. I began to appreciate the qualities and abilities I had and how I could use them to help others.

What are some of the qualities or abilities that you have yet to tap into? Have you had opportunities to use those abilities where you shied away due to a lack of confidence? What are people saying? Sometimes we don't recognize our talents. There may be that one thing we do well that others are always telling us we should do. Now may be the time to search within ourselves and develop the confidence to try it.

What in your life are you willing to build up the confidence to try?

Day 12 – "Explore Other Interests"

It is a wonderful feeling when we finally decide to make necessary changes in our lives. We've made all of the necessary plans, and are now ready to begin the journey toward our passion and our purpose. We have been laser-focused about what we want to do and things seem to be slowly falling into place. We are finally in a "good space".

While things are going well and positive energy is flowing, it is a perfect time to explore other interests. What I mean is, tap into other things that are going to enhance your journey. This may include taking a Tai Chi class, reading a motivational book, or visiting your local museum. Activities like these create a balance that allows you expand your mind and tap into your creativity. Sometimes we can get so consumed with what we are doing, that we lose touch with the people and things going on around us. Every once and a while, we need to culturally "plug in", so we can stay socially connected.

Taking a little time to explore other interests can also help us expand or vision and purpose. We have ideas for what we want to do, but sometimes exposure to other interests can enhance those ideas. In your exploration, you may find that what you envisioned, may be something that someone else needs. It may be something or someone that you had not considered. This holds true in both your personal and professional life.

In business, you can research and explore what other businesses similar to yours are doing. You may get a few ideas through your research that you hadn't considered. In relationships, you can research a few meet-up groups to see if you can meet people who are interested in something you want to learn more about. In this age of technology, the choices are endless!

What other interests do you have that are worth exploring?

Day 13 – "Ask for Help"

Have you ever heard the phrase, "Pride leads to destruction"? When we are prideful, we feel as though we are in control and we don't need anyone to assist us in our journey. "We got this!" We know what we want and what we need and we don't have time to explain it. It is easier to just do it ourselves.

Prideful is something, I must confess, I was guilty of being for a long time. Pride and I were best friends. I was used to being the head of my household and handling everything that came with that responsibility. I was great at my job, so I trained and mentored others. I was the "go to" person among my friends. Whatever anyone needed I had it. Whenever anyone needed someone to talk to or confide in…I was your girl. For these reasons, I found it very hard to rely on others, because so many people relied on me.

I realized once I decided to leave my corporate job and focus on my business full-time, I was in unchartered territory. I was experiencing things I had never experienced before. I no longer had a steady income. I had no debt and suddenly had to rely on credit cards to sustain me. I had to apply for food stamps for the first time in my life. It was a humbling experience. I had to learn to ask for help. I had to learn to rely on others to help me as I transitioned. Most of all, I had to stop making excuses for why I didn't want to ask for help. I had to learn to accept the help and how to say "thank you" for it. It was a chalky pill that I had to learn to swallow.

Pride has a dual meaning. It can be both positive or negative. It is all about perspective. Choose to be proud of the things that you are doing to elevate yourself, but don't be so proud that you can't ask for the help you need to get there.

Don't allow pride to lead to your destruction!

Day 14 – "Stay The Course"

There will be some days when you will question why you even made the decision to make a life change. You may say things like, "What was I thinking?", "What made me think that I could do this?", "What does he/she see in me?", "Nobody is going to want to invest their money in my business?", "I'm too old for this!"

To compound this will be the naysayers. Those who will try to minimize your efforts or confirm your negative thoughts. Your proverbial "haters". They are always concerned with what you are doing so they can cast a critical eye and pick apart anything you do. They are saboteurs and will go to great lengths to undermine your success.

When you feel like you just want to give up…I encourage you to stay the course! Think back to why you decided to do what you are doing. Your "why" should be your motivation to keep going. What was that one thing that made you step out on faith in the first place? Tap back into your "why" to restore and renew your faith in your decision to make a change. Know that the feelings you are having are temporary. We feel them when it seems like nothing monumental is happening at the moment. These are simply growing pains that we have to experience in order to stretch beyond our limits.

We have to be very careful not to give people authority over our lives. Sometimes we allow others to say things that cut our spirit or cause us to doubt our abilities. Most of the time it is a person who is envious of our gifts and talents. This is why it is important to see where the comments and remarks are coming from. Are they coming from a reliable source that you or others respect? If not, take it with a grain of salt and push forward. When people challenge why you chose to make the decision you make, you should be able to express, without conviction why your passion or purpose is YOURS. This is YOUR personal journey. Don't just be on the path to your destiny….OWN IT!

Don't let others dissuade you. Own your "why"!

Day 15 – " ½ Way Point"

We are at the half-way point in this book...

ARE WE HAVING FUN YET!

In the midst of anything that we do, we have to remind ourselves not to take everything so seriously!

Learn to laugh at yourself!

Be silly!

Eat your favorite junk food. YOU KNOW YOU WANT IT!
(I'll follow you to the moon and back for Red Velvet Cheesecake!!!)

Crank up the music in your car and sing along!

Dance, Dance, Dance!!!

Get hugs and give kisses!

Smile!

Tell somebody you love them!

Lighten up! No one likes to be around someone who is always uptight!

Day 16 – "Encouragement"

1 Thessalonians 5:5 says, "Therefore encourage one another and build each other up." In the competitive society we live in, we have become more accustomed to seeing jealousy and backbiting taking place, over an encouraging or uplifting word. Tearing a person down in order to boost themselves up, has become the new social norm.

When we encourage one another, it gives us hope. When we have hope, we believe that things are possible. We are encouraged not to give up, knowing that things will get better and work in our favor. The person (s) who encourages us does four important things: they support us, listen to us, care about us and pray for us. These people may not be in our inner circle, but they can be acquaintances who we work with, worship with, or connect with in some form or fashion. They have had an opportunity to meet us and get to know our character. They believe in what we're doing and want to encourage us to keep going down the path we're going.

Take time to surround yourself with those individuals who will encourage you. And while you are being edified, take a moment to give a word of encouragement to someone too. We should be willing to see the things that differentiate us and encourage those qualities that makes each of us unique. Another way that we can encourage each other is to COLLABORATE. Everything that we do in life does not have to be a competition. Comparisons don't always have to be made. When we work together, we can encourage and motivate each other so we BOTH benefit from the experience. As Christians, we should be willing to be our brother's keeper and encourage each other to be our personal best.

Whatever you do, be encouraged and DON'T QUIT!

Day 17 – "Take a Day Off"

We work hard to make sure that the changes in our lives receive the attention they deserve. Whether it is a new career, entrepreneurship or a new relationship, we put forth the effort we feel is necessary to make things work. We wake up early, go to bed late, miss meals and say "yes" far more often than we should, all in an effort to achieve our goals. As with everything, however, we need to take some time to recharge and regroup. When we push ourselves too hard for too long, our bodies and mental capacities begin to shut down. Then we are forced to take a break because we have no other choice.

Scheduling periodic days off allows for a more substantive time of restoration. Isn't it better to spend time doing things that fulfill us, rather than healing or recovering from our ailments? How much better would we feel after a day at the spa or curling up with a good book? How about catching a good movie or eating at your favorite restaurant? When we plan for these types of activities, it gives us something to look forward to. If our transition is career-based, a day off can serve as a reward for all of the hard work we have done. If our transition is relationship-based, a day off can be that "me time" we need every now and then.

You would be amazed at what a few planned days off each month can do for you, your business or your relationships. This time should be stress free. Try to complete tasks and be sure that those who may be effected by your day off, are aware that you will be unavailable. And when you say you are unavailable, BE UNAVAILABLE! Send your calls to voicemail and place your emails on auto-response. Enjoy your time off and make it your OWN!

Sorry. I unavailable at this time. Please leave a message…Beep!

Day 18 – "Live Authentically"

    To live an authentic life, means being true to who you are. You are true to your personality and spirituality. You have reached a level of self-consciousness where you have chosen to be "in this world, but not of this world". Despite any external forces or pressures, you choose to live your life on your terms. Living an authentic life is a beautiful space to be in because it is unique and tailor-made just for YOU!

    People who are authentic can be pleasant to be around because they are like a breath of fresh air. They are not pretentious or judgmental. They don't have a problem with expressing themselves and not easily swayed by those who may not agree with their philosophies. They truly see the beauty and uniqueness in others and support them accordingly. They are rare to find as friends, but when you do find them, they tend to be your friends for a lifetime.

    As you go through transitions in your life and are clear about the direction you are going in, stay true to that belief. Walk in what you know blesses you. Embrace what gives you joy and minimizes stress. You will find that others will be attracted to you because the aura you emit, is one of peace. Your spirit is calm and those around you can sense it. The confidence that comes with authenticity makes it possible for you to succeed because you have learned to ACCEPT YOURSELF. You are no longer driven by the desire to be accepted by others. Your focus becomes the epitome of self-love and self-worth.

Are you living an authentic life?

Day 19 – "Money Matters"

Money matters. It is one of those stressors that will make us abandon our dreams or not even consider them at all. When we are in financial distress, it can affect how and when transitions occur in our lives. Even when we take the steps to prepare for transitions financially, the unexpected can occur. A financial expense like an automobile, a home repair or an unexpected hospital bill can arise and take what seemed to be nice nest egg down to a negative balance. We can run out of money before we reach our anticipated goals. And then we may have to do, what for some, seems like the unthinkable. We may have to ASK FOR HELP!

Pride or the thought that the person we ask to help us financially, will keep this debt dangling over our heads, is more than some of us can bear. It is enough to make us want to give up and revert back to what is "safe and familiar", just so we don't have to ask for help or accrue any more expenses. It is a difficult space to be in when we feel we have to rely on others for our well-being, especially when we are accustomed to being independent. Money issues can lower our self-esteem and strain our relationships both professionally and personally. When we get to this point, what can we do?

The one thing you don't want to do is ignore the debt. If finances are becoming an issue, seek advice on how to prioritize your debt before it consumes you. Try to keep your routines in place and modify them if possible. If you have to limit your travel time in the car, due to limited funds for gas, try to consolidate and time your trips so they are in the same proximity and can be made in one trip. Phone a friend. Tap into the social services available in your area, if necessary. Learn to be resourceful. More importantly, don't give up on your passions and purpose. Make the necessary adjustments, realizing that what you are going through is only for a season. Sometimes being a little uncomfortable will push you to work a little harder to reach your goals.

Money matters. Learn to be resourceful and seek counsel when necessary.

Day 20 – "In the Zone"

    A great way to get "in the zone" and stay there is to set small, attainable goals. When we begin to successfully meet our goals and our confidence builds, we are more willing to take risks that we typically wouldn't. Fear and doubt are minimized and faith and confidence take their place.

    Following up with and keeping current on things relevant to your business or career, will keep you in the zone. Learning new concepts can get your creative juices flowing. You can add your spin to an existing concept that may make your business stand out from the rest. Connecting and collaborating with the right people can take your business to a higher level. Being in the zone and operating in it can be the difference between being a business owner and an industry leader.

    Having the desire to try new things in your relationship can keep you in the zone as well. Planning date nights, or spicing things up in the bedroom can spark romantic flames that may have been flickering out. Being present and giving your significant other your undivided attention, shows that you care, are interested, and still in love. Being in the zone and operating in it can be the difference between dating and marriage or a happy marriage and a pending divorce.

    The awesome thing about being in the zone is that feeling of momentum. You feel like nothing is going to stop you! Take the steps to stay there. When you begin to feel like things are tapering off, start looking for new things to get you back there. And when you finally run out of ideas, don't be afraid to ask those who you trust, for suggestions.

Get in the zone!

Day 21 – "Letting Go"

If we want to have the most success making transitions in our lives, we have to be willing to let go. Let go of old habits and negative thoughts. Let go of toxic people. Let go of the fear of failure or the fear of rejection. There are also things that we have to let go of, not for our good, but for the good of the other party involved. When we let go, we release those things that had us bound and open ourselves to receive those positive energies that will renew and restore us.

Letting go, however, is easier said than done. This is especially true when we have invested time in the person or thing that we have to let go of. I think of the time when I empty-nested. As a mother, I was involved in my children's activities. I was the cook, nurse, counselor and chauffer, among other things. Our role as parents never ends, but it changes. I had to learn to let go of my oldest daughter so that I didn't enabled her. I had to allow her to be her own person and make mistakes, knowing that I would be there to support her when necessary.

Letting go of toxic people has proven to be difficult as well. We can get caught up into thinking that we are helping the person who is toxic in our lives, instead of seeing that they are doing more harm to us than good. We have compensated for the things that are going on in their lives by appearing to "rescue" them. We tend to feel that they "need" us. That is where the toxicity begins and where we need to let go.

Negative thoughts take root from seeds that have been planted in our minds by ourselves or others. We can be hard on ourselves. When others confirm our negative thoughts, we take ownership of what was said. It becomes our truth. When we find fault with ourselves, we should seek to find ways to correct those things, <u>if</u> they are true. Those who will tell us about our shortcomings, should be coming with love, not malice in their hearts. We should be able to clearly know the difference. We have to be careful not to let people have so much authority over our lives that they change our mindset and have us walking in negativity. No one should ever be allowed to challenge your self-worth. That is a soul tie worth letting go of.

    Fear can be the hardest of all things to let go of. It can be paralyzing. It keeps us from believing we can do the things we set out to accomplish. It keeps us from even trying. Fear becomes that thing we hide behind when we feel we may be rejected by others. Fear is supposed to be a defense mechanism used to protect us from eminent danger. It was not designed to be an emotion that we use when we don't want to do something outside of our comfort zone. We have to be willing to conquer fear and not be afraid to blaze trails that haven't been made before. Those who conquer fear are some of the most innovative people of our time. Without them, we would not have any of the modern advances we have. Could you imagine a world where no one did anything because they were afraid to? We would be stuck in a time warp.

    Letting go also applies to those who have faith, hence the term "LET GO AND LET GOD". We have to be willing to be people of faith who pray and ask God's grace, mercy and favor over the things we are trying to accomplish. Then we can rest in knowing that God has our best interest and will bless those things we are doing in His name. We can then begin praising Him and thanking Him for all that He has done and will do. All we have to do is let go!

Let it go! Don't hold it back anymore!

Day 22 – "Being Present"

How many times have you gone to a meeting or out to dinner with a friend or loved one, and the person seemed preoccupied the entire time? They appeared to be distracted by their phone or thoughts. Their body language lets you know that they are in another place far from where you are. You begin to wonder what you are doing there?

In this age of technology and accessibility, it is easy to feel obliged to be available to everyone at all times. We have almost been conditioned to believe that we are not connected if we don't have our technological devices by our sides. How many times have you turned around to go back home because you left your phone? What about that feeling you have when your phone is about to die and you either left your charger or can't find an available outlet to charge it? I have seen people, young and old, experience total meltdown without their electronic devices. It is disheartening.

While it is wonderful to have the convenience of technology, we have to remember that all good things should be used in moderation. It is great to be able to reach someone in an emergency or to have a reminder of appointments we have or calls we have to make. But when we schedule time to meet with someone whether it be for business or pleasure, we should at least be willing to make that time, quality time. We should be willing to put our phones away and be present with the one we are connecting with.

Being present is a powerful thing. Both you and the person you are with will reap the benefits when you take the time to show interest. You both get to experience the intentions of your time together and can walk away replenished.

Being PRESENT allows you to see the important things you may miss when you're not paying attention.

Day 23 – "Nobody Can Be You"

      If there is one thing I want you to remember when transitioning, it is this: Making a transition in your life, does NOT mean losing your IDENTITY. Just because we are doing something new, doesn't mean we have to change who we are. Our goal should be to enhance our lives, not to completely depart from it. Nobody can be you. You were uniquely designed to be who you are and to fulfill the purpose you were put on this earth to achieve.

      Understand, however, that your identity will be challenged and even shaken by the naysayers and by your own sense of self. This is when you have to look in the mirror and see those qualities that lie within you that scream, "YES I CAN!" It was the desire deep inside of you that made you decide to make a change. There may have been others who influenced you, but it was YOU who received that information, and chose to act on it.

      Now with change, may come a change in the roles that you play. You may take on the role of a wife/husband or a boss or an entrepreneur. This may require you to attain new skills to be successful in your new role. You should be building on a foundation that already exists. It should be a practice of broadening your base in an effort to stretch and grow beyond the areas you have been comfortable in.

      Anything that is going to completely change who you are, may be worth reconsidering. When you are seeking to discover the passion and purpose for your life, it comes from within. It does not exist in the unfamiliar. It is the reawakening of something that is familiar only to you. Think of it in terms of your AHA moment. You recognize it when you hear it, because it was always there. Don't lose who you are. Discover what's inside of you.

Nobody can be you. Embrace who you are through your transition.

Day 24 – "Don't Recreate the Wheel"

Have you heard this term before; "Don't recreate the wheel". If what we are doing is working, keep doing it. As we transition, there may be habits or qualities that we have that are beneficial. I remember when I decided to write my first book entitled *"30 Days of Inspiration, "From the Sideline…."* I was so worried about what the book was going to be about. I had written little nuggets of inspiration every day, for over a month. I had over 45 nuggets written, but couldn't figure out what to write about!

I was trying to recreate the wheel. I had already created nuggets of inspiration that were posted every day on Facebook and they were well received by those who read them. Why did I think I had to do something different? It was then that I realized my book was already written! All I needed to do was add a few touches to it and the next thing I knew I was a published author. I would have ever written my book, because I thought I had to do "more". With several copies of my book sold, I'm glad I followed my heart and did it!

As you transition, be sure to use your strengths. If you are creative, use that creativity as you transition. If you are a good manager of your time, incorporate that into your daily routine as you transition. There will be plenty of opportunities to develop new concepts and skills during your journey. Expand those talents when you need to. Otherwise, keep doing those things that are working for you.

Transitioning can include building on what already exists. Take the time to research your interests and find creative and innovative ways to make it work for you. A little initiative can go a long way!

Don't recreate the wheel. Make it a vehicle and watch it go!

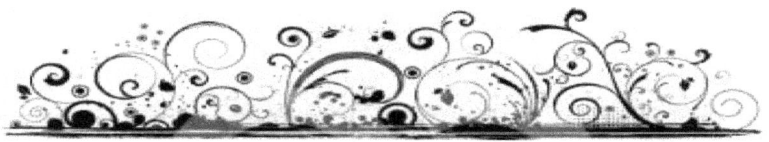

Day 25 – "Write Your Own Chapter"

With all of the emotions that transitions take us through, have you ever considered documenting it? Your journey could be the motivation that others need to take the leap of faith necessary to change their lives. We all have a story to tell. Stories of love, victory, grief, failure, success and triumph. There may be a lesson or a word of inspiration we didn't know was relevant to someone else's life. Why not share it?

Writing our story is not just an opportunity to share our experiences with others. It is also a way for us to purge those things that may be heavy on our hearts. It can be therapeutic for both you and the person receiving your message. When we write from our heart and allow the words to flow, we can discover messages that we have for ourselves that needed to come out. We can re-read our story and be empowered and inspired by our own words!

Writing about the next chapter in your life, especially if you are making a significant change, can provide a time line of gratitude. When you can reflect on the highs and lows you are experienced, you can appreciate the journey even more. You may realize that there were so many more victories you experienced than defeats. We tend to magnify the negative experiences we have. We need to learn to celebrate the positive experiences as well. Most of life's lessons are learned in the midst of adversity, but it is okay to write about how choosing to live a victorious life has enhanced the quality of your life. No matter what your story is…WRITE IT!

Think about the legacy you would be leaving for your family and generations to come. Once your story is written, no one can take that experience from you. Your words become life, FOREVER.

Consider authoring the next chapter of YOUR LIFE.

Day 26 – "Be a Person of Integrity"

It is very important to me, both personally and professionally, to be a woman of integrity. The bible says in Philippians 4:8, "Finally, brothers, whatever is true, whatever is honorable, whatever is just, whatever is pure, whatever is lovely, whatever is commendable, if there is any excellence, if there is anything worthy of praise, think about these things."

We should all strive to be people of integrity. No one should have to second guess what your intentions are. With integrity comes trust. If someone can trust you, your relationship with them will thrive because your character is not in question. They know that they can depend on you to do what you say you're going to do. It is a good feeling when we can be that person that others have no problem referring or supporting.

Integrity is important, especially if you are a business owner. As a coach, my integrity represents me, my business and my partner. We are not selling products. We are providing a service. We want our clients to come back to us because they trust us and see the value of our services. We represent our business with excellence and that starts with integrity.

The same holds true with your personal relationships. Your spouse or significant other should know that you are committed to your relationship and that you respect them by being faithful. You should be willing to communicate with them in truth. Integrity will create the intimate relationships you desire. We should seek to do good by others daily. The reward of being a person of integrity is FAVOR. You will experience the desires of your heart when you choose to conduct yourself with integrity. More importantly, remember that it is your ACTIONS, not your words that make you a person of integrity.

Life a life of integrity and you will prosper.

Day 27 – "Experience Gratitude"

Living a life of gratitude can be transformative. When we take the time to express gratitude for the things that we have been blessed to experience, it changes our perspective. It can turn a stressful situation into one that will give you peace. How? This is what works for me…

Each morning I wake up, I say my prayers and thank God for the breath of life. I thank him for my health and for shelter and utilities and food to eat. I thank him for my family and friends and for their health and wellbeing. I express gratitude in preparation for all that God has for me that day. It is a time of thanksgiving and fellowship with Almighty God. It gives me peace. Once I have done this, I write down my intentions for the day so my day has direction. I then meditate so that I can center myself for the day's activities. Then I do some form of exercise so that I can prepare my body as well.

When my day is over, I take out my gratitude journal and write down three things that I was thankful for. When I first started keeping a gratitude journal, there were some days when I stared at the blank page, not knowing what I was going to write. I couldn't see anything positive after a stressful day. But over time, this practice allowed me to reflect on the small things that I could be grateful for. I realized that I could find something to be grateful for even on my most challenging days. It is another opportunity for me to express gratitude and to end my day with the peace it started with. I am able to sleep with a clear conscious.

Consider this a gratitude challenge: Start a gratitude journal today and see how it will change your mindset. See how the blessings in your life will manifest themselves because you took the time to give thanks. When we experience gratitude we open ourselves up to receive more things in our lives to be grateful for. Experience gratitude while you are transitioning and see how it will transform you.

Are you ready to participate in the gratitude experience?

Day 28 - "RedeFINDing You"

In the midst of our transition, we can sometimes lose our way. Think of it as your internal GPS system. You have an idea of where you would like to go, you just don't quite know how to get there. Every turn you seem to take, turns out to be another dead end. You feel like you are in a constant state of "recalculating". This is when you need to "pull over", get your bearings and restart your internal GPS.

RedeFINDing you means rediscovering and repurposing your life. It is reigniting that fire inside of you to want to pursue forgotten dreams. It is remembering what your goals and aspirations were before they took a back seat to the current roles you play in other people's lives. RedeFINDing you is coming back to center and aligning with your authentic self.

The journey to redeFINDing you is riddled with emotional highs and low as it requires you to take a hard look at yourself and to ask yourself some tough questions. It requires you to look at your past, in order to design the path for your future. It requires you to face past hurts and fears in order to experience breakthroughs. In the end, you will be left with the coordinates toward your passion and purpose, and can now merge back into your life with focus and direction.

As a Life Empowerment coach, I have been blessed to help individuals calibrate their internal GPS systems. I have seen them thrive as they took the wheel, stepped on the gas, and drove confidently toward their destiny. It is an amazing ride when you have a destination. The road isn't easy, but once you reach your destination, you will see that it was worth the trip!

Where will the new coordinates of your life take YOU?

Day 29 – "The Manifestation"

When we are going through a transition, we eventually get to a point where the changes we have made begin to manifest themselves. The changes become more evident. We have transitioned to a space that no longer looks the space we were in before. Our confidence level has grown and we are operating with a renewed mindset. Doubt and fear may still be present, but they have become a small voice in the corner of our minds that no longer get our full attention. Our transition is ending and our transformation is beginning.

Earlier this year, I took a leap of faith and left my corporate job. I wanted to pursue my coaching business, as well as obtain my doctoral degree. I had big plans and the confidence to make these goals come into fruition. I knew it would be a tough journey, but I felt prepared. As I drove out of the parking lot of my job for the last time, I felt a new sense of excitement and hope for my future. I knew that in time, my efforts would manifest themselves and I would achieve my passion and purpose.

What manifested first were my fears and anxieties as things didn't initially go as planned. At my lowest point, I ran out of savings and had to apply for food stamps. I had to take on side jobs to supplement my income so I would not lose my home or have my utilities cut off. I acquired debt after being debt-free for 14 years. This was not the manifestation I expected, but it was the one I received. When I really began to get laser-focused about my business, eventually things began to manifest in my business and things improved.

Manifestations are a result of the things happening around us, so we need to be careful about where our focus is. When we focus in on those areas in our lives where we want to see manifestations, with time they will materialize.

With manifestation comes transformation. Are you ready?

Day 30 – "Transformation"

You've made it! You took all of the steps necessary to make a major transition in your life. You've gone through the preparation and planning. You've taken the leap of faith. You've have traveled the uncharted course and paved the path to your destiny. It wasn't easy, but it was WORTH IT! You are finally at the point where you are beginning to see the fruits of your labor. The manifestations are evident. A renewing of your mind has taken place. The transition is over and now the transformation begins…

As a teenager, I loved the Transformers cartoon. Optimus Prime was my favorite. I thought it was so cool to see each character change from a vehicle to a robot. What a concept to be able to see something transform right before your eyes. While their transformations took place in an instant, our transformations take a little bit longer. The changes may not be noticed right away, but we hope that others will see that something is different.

To transform means to make a dramatic change outwardly or in character or condition. Once a transformation has taken place in our lives, we can begin to walk in its truth. We become US…only better. We have successfully transitioned to where we wanted to be. We may experience setbacks from time to time, but we are in a different space now. We can make minor adjustments and still continue to move forward.

So what now? We get ready for *30 Days of Transformation "From the Sideline… - Walking in Our Truth*! The path to our past is behind us and we can continue to blaze a path toward the new goals and purpose that lie ahead. Until then…

You've made the transition. Start living your transformed life!

"Breaking the Boundaries of Love and Life"

Visit our website www.unlimitedloveandlife.com

Like Us on Facebook www.facebook/unlimitedloveandlife

Follow Us on Twitter www.twitter.com/loveunlimitedco

Follow Our Blog Talk Radio Show
www.blogtalkradio.com/loveunlimited

Kim M. Martin & Sheronda L. Barksdale are Life Empowerment Coaches, Authors and Professional Speakers
They are the Co-Founders of Unlimited Love and Life Coaching, LLC and the Co-Hosts of the Blog Talk Radio Show, "Love Unlimited: Relationship Coaching with Kim and Sheronda"

Visit their website to schedule your coaching session, workshop or public speaking engagement TODAY!

Visit www.amazon.com/author/kimmmartin
to purchase my latest books online.

www.ingramcontent.com/pod-product-compliance
Lightning Source LLC
Chambersburg PA
CBHW051712090426
42736CB00013B/2665